THE

DESPICABLE

MISSIONARY

How a Young Christian Girl in Pakistan
Learned to Defend her Faith and Love
Muslims

By Annie Bradley with Julie Dass

Study Guide
By Tim Nickel

The Despicalbe Missionary Study Guide

1. ISBN 978-0-9966779-7-4

Mission Nation Publishing, Naples, FL

Tim Nickel is a Lutheran Pastor and Missionary. After graduating from Concordia Seminary, St. Louis, MO, in 1970, Tim served as a parish pastor of congregations in Gowanda NY, Scranton PA, Ridley Park PA, and Hamlin NY for twenty-eight years. After their four children had graduated high school and left home, Tim and Marguerite sensed a call to foreign missionary work to plant churches in unreached territory. In 1998 The Lutheran Church – Missouri Synod called Tim to be Evangelistic Missionary to the newly independent country of Kyrgyzstan in Central Asia. After overseeing the start of over 50 churches in Kyrgyzstan, the Nickels lived in Turkey for two years, retiring and repatriating to St. Augustine, Florida in 2009.

Introduction

Our daily prayer is "Forgive us our trespasses, as we forgive those who trespass against us." Receiving the forgiveness of sin by grace through faith because of Jesus Christ gives us the certain hope of eternal life. But there's more! Giving the forgiveness of sins to those who have hurt and offended us is vital to living out the Christian faith in daily life. *Receiving and giving forgiveness completes the circle of life with God.*

Forgiveness, both receiving and giving, is a life lesson that the Holy Spirit teaches every believer. No child of God will live long before opportunities to learn love and acceptance from God and for others come along. Sometimes these lessons will be extremely difficult learning processes, but very valuable. Learning forgiveness strengthens faith and character, develops patience and kindness, overcomes anger and resentment, replaces hatred with love, and smooths interpersonal relations so that we may become credible witnesses to Jesus Christ.

One hard lesson for most human beings is learning to love, accept and forgive people who are different than we are. Another hard lesson is learning how to respond to rejection and to those who mistreat us because we are different. Learning to live like Jesus is lifelong process. He did not tolerate sin but He loved the sinner. Christians will not tolerate sinful behavior either, in themselves or in others, but they will always love and accept the person who sins. Only the Holy Spirit can teach this attitude, through God's Word and in the school of experience.

Forgiveness of sins is central to Christian faith and life.

The book *The Despicable Missionary* immerses us in the life of Victoria, the Christian girl from Pakistan whose story relates her experiences dealing with anger and forgiveness in another culture. As we read her experiences, we empathize with her feelings of rejection for being different or even inferior, her anger for being unfairly and unjustly mistreated, and her reaction to being unexplainably persecuted for being a Christian. We will ask, "How can she forgive such trespassers?" Our next question should be, "How can God forgive me my trespasses? "It is then that we realize the challenge—and power—of total forgiveness and unconditional love.

Forgiveness comes from love and produces love. Faith in the Gospel and the love of God inspires and compels us and makes it possible to love others.

Loving those who love us is not so hard; loving those who hate us, bully us, say bad things about us, unjustly accuse us, act as enemies, and persecute us is hard. Victoria's story puts us inside such challenging situations and helps us ask hard questions for our lives, too.

Loving those who are like us is not so hard; loving those whose worldview, culture, language, politics, class, and even race are not like us is very hard. We don' t understand "them" and cannot relate to "them." To accept strangers as human beings like us for whom Christ died may sometimes seem a barrier too high. Most people have a blind spot in regard to their own prejudices against people who are different from themselves, and it is all too easy unconsciously to see them as inferior. The Holy Spirit is constantly teaching us in Word and Sacrament to recognize our own issues with diverse persons and to see them as persons whom God loves. Only God can lead us to understand, forgive, accept and love people who are afraid of us or whom we are afraid of. Studying and applying the lessons that Victoria learned can be used now by the Holy Spirit to open our eyes.

Session One: Being Despicable

The Prologue narrates what happened to Talib Syed, grandfather of Victoria, when he was disowned by his father and exiled from the family because he became a Christian. Talib knew he would suffer persecutions from his neighbors within the country of Pakistan, which is predominantly Muslim. He was prepared for that. He determined that with the help of Jesus he would overcome hatred with love.

He resolved to pass the love of Jesus on to succeeding generations, that his children and grandchildren would learn to replace their hatred with love. This is the lesson that Talib's granddaughter would have to learn the hard way, and that story becomes the theme of the book.

Chapter 1: "Despicable"

As a child, Victoria was called *paleed*, despicable. She was despicable in the eyes of her playmates and neighbors because she was a Christian. This designation of Christian was not just religious, although that was a part of it. The real issue is a result of the old "caste system" inherited from the Hindu religion. To be Christian was not even a low class; Christians were considered even lower. They were "outcasts." This classification was based on a so-called *zat*, a kind of classification of humans that was determined by arbitrary means of separating people into various strata of society. Victoria began to realize how the culture she lived in regarded her, just because she was Christian.

Despicable is a translation of *paleed* to describe the lowest of the low, people who were considered barely human. What other English words have you heard to describe such a class? In your community? Have you heard such a term used against someone or against yourself? What is their/your the reaction?

Why can you sympathize with Victoria's reaction?

How would you describe the issue that Victoria needed to deal with?

What was she told was the proper Christian response?

Have you ever told children to "turn the other cheek" to a bully? What was the result?

Chapter 2: "A Father's Lesson"

Victoria learned from her father that in the Pakistani culture Christians are considered the lowest class. She learned that in that culture Muslins cannot treat Christians well in any situation. She would have to learn to live with that.

At the top of page 9 is the generalization that people have a hard time accepting or understanding those who are different from themselves. This theme is fairly universal. Can you think of examples from our own culture in which American people have such a similar hard time?

What did the father tell his daughter that Christians must learn to forgive? What did Jesus forgive from the cross (Luke 23:34)?

What do you think of the father's statement on page 10 ("If we are asked, we should never deny who we are, but we don't need to go out of our way to say so.")?

We are getting a glimpse into the character of Victoria, dealing with issues like anger, pride, stubbornness, and such. Her father says, "God made her different (page 11)." How is that true? How is that an excuse?

Chapter 3: "The Outcast"

Another incident at school brought up the taunts of *paleed*, despicable, because she was a Christian. She could not understand what it was about being a Christian that made other children avoid her. She was considered an outcast. In Pakistani culture such treatment was considered acceptable and even deserved. Was "being a Christian" a cultural or a religious question? Does it matter?

Would you say what Victoria's mother said on the bottom of page 15, "Stand up for yourself when you are feeling persecuted, but do so peacefully." ? Is that sound advice? Is it Biblical?

Do you feel people fail to look at you "for what you are inside" ? When might this happen to you? How does that make you feel not to be "seen?"

Chapter 4: "She is a Child, just like you"

Paleed persecutions continued. Victoria decided she would fight. "If someone pushes you, push back..." (page 20). Pride and petulance were still problems for the growing girl. In your experience, how long might it take to learn the "forgiveness" lesson?

Can you explain the connections between fear and hate that, in this case, the Pakistani people exhibit? Why do people fear someone who is different? Is it because they threaten the culture and the beliefs that they are used to? Does fear lead to hate? Is it possible that people fear Christians? Why?

Chapter 5: "The Gifts of Christmas"

Victoria was beginning to understand the power of the Word of God, and she was eager to read and use the Word to influence other people.

One Christmas she received a smile from another boy and she received compliments on her portrayal of Mary. She also received a wonderful compliment from her beloved Christian grandfather: she was a good Christian. These positive experiences were strong motivations for Victoria: she promised to be a good Christian in Pakistan.

A positive word of encouragement and blessing can be a strong motivation to make a commitment and a promise. What else can timely encouragements prompt?

Session Two: Growth and Development

Chapter Six: "Sangla School"

Victoria was now in a new school where she had to learn new adjustments. It was a different experience for her to be away from home in a boarding house. She could not get used to the bed and the food. Her stubbornness wouldn't allow her to get comfortable in a new setting.

But eventually she learned that she could live among Muslim and Christian girls and, in time, familiarity with Scripture, the comfort of Christian music, and the apparent acceptance of her peers calmed her fears. A sense of belonging washed over her. What does it take to instill in you an important sense of belonging?

A sense of community, bonding, and commitment to the Christian faith on the part of her fellow students moved her to be comfortable. She felt she was not excluded. Is this what the Church is about? In which communities do you feel accepted? Not accepted? Why? For our own comfort and security, how important is it to be surrounded by people who are like us? Do you see value in exploring other communities? Why?

Chapter Seven: "There are consequences for your actions"

Victoria still has problems with sullenness, petulance and anger. This attitude led to an incident with other students who were injured by Victoria. She felt disrespected by some students but loved and respect her teacher and did not want to displease her.

She still had issues with Muslims, but then in a conversation with her beloved grandfather she learned that he was once a Muslim, until he converted to Christianity. Would she have loved him the same as a Muslim as she did as a Christian?

In your experience, if acquaintances left the religion in which they were raised, did you love them more or less? Does a person's faith affect your respect and love for them? How does a person's ethnic origin or sexual orientation affect your respect and love?

Why is it easier to love those who think and act like us? And why so we tend to be fearful of those who are different? What persons can you recall in the New Testament who either taught or learned acceptance of persons different from ourselves? (See Luke 7:1-10; John 4:7-29; Acts 10.)

Victoria was learning to forgive the ignorance of others. She was even learning to forgive Muslim children who insulted her (page 41). But she got into another scrape with a boy who wouldn't treat a girl equally.

Can you see that being on the receiving end of prejudice is like being unfairly accused? Can anyone stand being rejected for no good reason? Which is more important to you: being loved or being respected?

Chapter 8: "Disgrace"

Victoria was betrothed by family contract to William at a young age. She accepted that arrangement within her culture and was even looking forward to the marriage. But then something terrible happened, something that disgraced her and her family: William broke the engagement because he felt she was too young. This was a devastating rejection for her once again, and in Pakistani culture it was one of the worst things that can happen.

However, this "last straw" enabled her to resolve that she could and would change. Something good came out of this bad situation. But it seems that God was working something even better for her: now Victoria was going to go to high school and pursue an education.

Have you experienced great loss or disappointment or tragedy? Does God really work all things together for good to them that love Him?

Is it easy to believe God's promises? Why?

Chapter 9: "A New Opportunity"

Victoria was going to the big city of Lahore and leave home, an unusual experience (for a woman). She had learned to have a more gracious outlook toward people of different religions. (page 53). Are people like Victoria sheltered from the ignorance and prejudices of people more in urban or rural communities?

Victoria caught the insight that all people were created in a unique way with all sorts of differences from each other, but each one was the same inside with an equal amount of love. (page 54) What have you found is the same and what is different about the many people, all created by God, whom you have met?

It seems as though the choice between marriage at age 14, as was normal for Pakistani girls, or continuing her education was made for her by circumstances. Do you think she should see God's hand in this, and that God's will was being done?

Chapter 10: "An unexpected acceptance"

Grandfather Talib converted from Islam to Christianity, but in the process lost his family and a way of life and entered into a whole new life! Why did he make that break?

The story of Talib's spiritual journey begins with the need to learn English and the desire for an education. So he shocked the family by joining the British military during the War. He later learned why he had this desire and did such a thing, for after joining the British army he became a Christian. Do you think the Lord had a hand in this choice? Does God work in mysterious ways, or what?

Lesson Three: Conversion and Bridges

Chapter 11: "My Brother"

Talib's conversion to Christianity came through the friendship of a Christian man. Converting to Christ was the most difficult and courageous thing he had ever done. Talib had questions and was not satisfied with the answers in the Quran. Through his new British friend he came to a different understanding of prayer. How would you describe the difference in prayer practice between Talib and Major John (page 62)?

His friend gave Talib a Bible, which ultimately became the means of convincing and converting him. His friendship with Major John was solidified and sealed when he saved his life. How did this even bond them together so closely?

Chapter 12: "An Unexpected Invitation"

Talib read the Bible that his friend had given him. Reading the Bible opened his heart to Jesus' words. Then he was invited to a dinner meal with Major John, who began the meal with prayer in Jesus' name. Talib was so offended that he could not eat the meal set before him. Why did Talib not permit himself to partake in this meal together? (page 69) Can you understand his feelings?

How did Major John respond to Talib's sensibilities?

To remove the offense Talib invited Major John to his house for dinner, but what would his father think about having a Christian man in his home?

Chapter 13: "A Bridge is Begun"

The shared meal at Talib's house exhibited the differences between the two cultures and religions. What issues were raised?

Talib told his father that Major John was different. His father simply said he was an infidel no matter how nice he is. In what way was Major John different? (page73)

Talib kept reading the Bible. What did he learn about God from the Bible?

He also learned that because of God' s love for us we also love one another. We can learn to love everyone, and we can learn to forgive anyone who hurts us (page 74). What did he say happens when people choose not to understand one another?

Victoria was challenged to create a bridge of understanding between Christians and Muslims in her life. Creating a bridge of understanding became a part of her mission in life. Can you see the possibility of something like that becoming a part of your mission? How can we create understanding between different people? Why doesn't it seem easy? Is it possible?

Chapter 14: "Building the Bridge"

A bridge of understanding between Christians and Muslims could not be built unless they would work to accept one another. Victoria would seek understanding through education (page 76). What course did she take to become educated?

Victoria got into an argument about Jesus being the Son of God. The conflict between what the Bible says and what the Quran says is essential. How could she know which authority is right?

As angry as she felt Victoria was able to control her emotions and avoid a violent argument. She began to be at peace with herself while she was free to ask the questions her curiosity demanded. It helped that she had Christian friends who believed, thought, and enjoyed the same things. This atmosphere helped feel comfortable to pursue her studies of Christianity and Islam. Has your thinking changed about how important it is for us to live within our comfort zone among people who are like us? Why?

From within the comfort and security of our fellowship with other Christians we might be able to move out of our comfort zone and engage with others who are different. Is the building of bridges an intentional effort, or will it happen automatically?

Chapter 15: "Nationalization"

In 1977, Bhutto was deposed as leader of Pakistan, and Zia became the ruler. What was the significance of this coup?

Along with religious intolerance in the land, the culture shifted to the more traditional ways of living as opposed to Western ways. The girls were told to "be quiet, accept, understand."

Victoria was growing in her education, especially in Islamic studies, and she became the head girl and she would lead the morning announcements. Muslim prayers were allowed at the school, but what was that she was not allowed to do? (page 83-84)

Victoria was still dealing with anger arising from the unfair treatment of women and Christians. Learning to deal with a strong-willed personality can take a lifetime. But is it easy or hard to sympathize with Victoria?

Just when she was maturing and growing as a Christian, things were changing in Pakistan for Christians. And it would soon get even worse.

Lesson   Four: Persecutions Increase

Chapter 16: "The Protests Begin"

Victoria saw evidence of a new culture in Pakistan in the *burqa* worn by her mother. The unrest and unpredictability on Lahore was palpable. And then there was self-immolation of the Bhutto supporter. Unruly mobs were always possible. Everyone was becoming fearful and the threat of violence was on the rise.

How do you explain the question Victoria asked, "Are culture and religion becoming the same law"? And what does that mean?

It was getting harder and harder to forgive those who created new laws, especially those laws that threatened to hurt or kill Christians (page 89). The temptations to rise up in anger were once again beginning to overwhelm. Can you blame Victoria for refusing to forgive and giving place to anger?

What activity did she engage in to soothe the hatred (page 89)?

Chapter 17: "Pursuit"

Jamat E Islami is the angry movement that was seeking "complete Islam," that is, seeking to change morality, politics, law and culture to conform only to Islam and to exclude western influences. This means any religion outside of Islamic culture is subject to persecution. Victoria's bubbling hatred for Muslims made her no better than they were.

One day the men from Jamat E Islami chased the girls of the school, threw rocks, insulted them, and tried to harm them. After and hour long attack of threats and violence the members of Jamat E Islami finally got tired and left.

Victoria was injured in this attack, and she was happy to be alive and grateful that she was not raped. What could happen to a woman and her family in this culture if she were raped (page 96-97)?

What do you imagine happens if one simply stifles one's own indignation and anger at such evil and violence?

In your experience, is it easy to separate the evil from the groups that do such things? What peoples in the more recent past can you think of who have been challenged in this way? How is it possible to still love the individuals while condemning their actions?

Chapter 18: "Whom Can we Trust?"

While Victoria finished high school, life in Pakistan to be in turmoil. Living quietly in fear was the new normal. More protests erupted. Many were slaughtered just for being labeled "infidels." Her father said, "We live in controversial times. The best we can do is remain quiet, live our lives and remain faithful to Jesus." (page 100) Do you think this was the best advice? Why?

What did they use as a guide for living their lives during those times?

The Quran does require different punishments for Muslims and infidels. Does the Quran teach Muslims that it is OK literally to use their swords to kill, or is this one interpretation?

Is the claim that the Quran teaches that killing an infidel, such as a Christian, is rewarded with a paradise of 72 virgins true or false? Is this the meaning of the Quran or an illegitimate interpretation? How could we find out, considering that Islam had no central authority on interpretation of the Quran?

Women are powerless in Muslim Pakistan. Education is discouraged. Women are only servants of the patriarch. Some Muslims are trying to force these kinds of cultural beliefs into laws of the Islamic state. Are these the teachings of the Quran or are they hateful interpretations of Islamist extremists?

Will these kinds of laws deprive communities of excellent education and health care?

When looking through Muslim eyes, Christians are infidels (page 103). Would this kind of thinking make you angry, too?

Chapter 19: "At Attempt at Conversion"

A house cleaner or "sweeper" was from a lower class and regarded as unclean, even filthy and contaminated. Victoria's experience with their Christian and kindly house cleaner taught her a new lesson. Her grandmother, however, had scolded her for touching the sweeper. What effect did the stories of Jesus healing the leper and other outcasts help Victoria?

Victoria was still learning much about treating people of a different class and even how to treat people of a different religion or culture. In the process, Victoria's anger welled up once again.

What is a *chaddar* (page 109)? Why did she have to wear it to continue in college?

Chapter 20: "An Offense"

At college Victoria found the Muslim teachers and students to be very intolerant of her and her beliefs. What did they find offensive on her (page 115)?

What did she find offensive about them?

She began to study the Bible more and more as well as continuing her studies of Islam, and her questions and curiosity still grew. However, she still angered easily. Victoria's father, Ishaq, thought it would be good for her to go to United Bible Theological College for the summer, hopefully to help manage her anger.

Lesson Five: Becoming a Missionary

Chapter 21: "A Faith Mission Revealed"

Victoria was very happy to be studying at United Bible Theological College. She fit in and took classes in training girls to become Bible Teachers.

What did she learn that helped her understand why Muslim youth were willing to martyr themselves (page 119)?

Many young Muslims discovered a feeling of love and acceptance in Islam. Isn't that the main reason most people are attached to any group at all? Think of growing up in either a loving family or in an abusive one; what might young persons from those backgrounds be looking for?

As Victoria learned about King David and about Saint Peter she saw that faith will keep you strong in life and in death.

She loved her grandfather for what lived inside him. This helped her understand not to judge peoples based on what we see on the outside. Victoria began to value looking beyond religious labels, skin tones, gender, age economic status to see what lives within.

What, then, would become her faith mission, her mission in life (page 123)?

Chapter 22: "In Mourning"

Victoria's summer studies at Bible College sustained her through college, and she became a well-educated woman in spite of Pakistani barriers to women.

After her mother died she learned again the importance of love, as her mother treated everyone with respect. What could the smallest token of kindness heal (page 125)?

The family believed that William's rejection of marriage led to her mother's death. Although Victoria was given another opportunity to be married, that proved to be an unacceptable match.

Chapter 23: "A Missionary"

Victoria was excited that she had taken a new job, teaching computer science at a school in Rawalpindi. One reason for her excitement was the opportunity for a Christian to teach Muslim students and cooperate with Muslim teachers. What did she feel that she was becoming (page 128)?

How is it possible for all of us the see ourselves as missionaries in whatever vocation God has placed us?

Victoria was ready for a servant future, and she trusted the Holy Spirit to empower her. She saw her mission opportunity with two Afghani students and their mother. The mother of Saqib and Abid told here that as refugees the family had lost everything and was now fearful of trusting anyone. But there was difference that she and the boys noticed in Victoria. This gave her the courage to ask Victoria to tutor the boys, so that they would not have to leave school. Her loving and tutoring paid off and they both improved in school.

What did this mother learn about Christians from this relationship (page 137)?

It seems that Victoria has learned to overcome hatred and fear by responding with love and kindness. How did Victoria handle her first missionary assignment? Love and kindness transcends all. Where in the New Testament do we read where this love comes from? (Romans 8:31-19; 1 John 3:20.)

Chapter 23 (b): "The Cross I Cannot Refuse"

Victoria was thankful that she was making a difference. Her Christian faith did not affect her career. She could grow above the prejudices she had suffered. For what reasons, in your opinion, does it sometimes takes a long time for the Holy Spirit to overcome anger, hatred and prejudice in people?

Victoria received a student's gift of cross earrings. She later learned that the mother had been to America and received the cross as a gift. As a Muslim, he could not wear them, but she took them anyway and gave them to a Christian. Victoria was disappointed that this bridge was not built. She said, "The cross you cannot accept, I cannot refuse."

When her father joined her mother in death, Victoria took the spiritual and cultural cross they had carried and made sure their message endured.

Chapter 24: "An Unknown Brother"

Victoria took a new job working with two Muslim men who actually treated her kindly and with respect. What did she learn about herself in this encounter?

Her new boss, Fazal, was very different than most Muslim men. Victoria expected him to see women only within the cultural divisions which Pakistani Muslims placed on themselves, seeing stereotypes instead of individuals.

She knew God was teaching her a lesson. Victoria had always tried to command respect. What did she learn about the right way to get respect (page 147)?

It was a long time coming, but she finally learned to respect Muslims. We can easily understand how difficult it was to learn that lesson.

Lesson Six: God Works all out for Good

Chapter 25: "The Lost Sheep"

To Victoria' s consternation and to our surprise she was now feeling like an outcast in her own Christian community but was feeling welcome in a women' s Islamic studies group. This was a time of some guilt and confusion for her, so she delved deeper into the Word of God, looking for peace and renewed faith. In serious prayer she felt that the Lord was speaking comfort and hope to her from the Word. What was the verse of Scripture that spoke to her heart (page 150)?

Chapter 26: "The Strength to Forgive"

When William, who had abandoned their engagement years before, showed up at her door asking forgiveness from her and her parents, she was shocked and anger boiled up within her once again. Conflicted, she wanted to punch him and embrace him at the same time.

William was simply asking for forgiveness, while explaining that he had rejected the marriage for *her* sake. She really was too young for marriage, he realized. Although he should have promised to fulfill the engagement in five years, he did not. This failure on his part caused much pain for her father and mother and for Victoria, and for this he sincerely apologized.

At the same time, Victoria had begun to learn about human rights outside of Pakistan and that the idea of a "child-bride" was a harmful cultural norm.

What was the outcome of William's request for forgiveness? How did Victoria resolve the issue of forgiving (page 155)?

One driving force that prompted her to actually forgive William was this question: What would forgiveness do to her faith mission? She finally found that she could forgive him. It seems that her faith mission was the most important factor in her ability to forgive. Her faith had given her a new voice, achieved through unconditional forgiveness. What was the unexpected result of her forgiveness, in regard to William (page 157)?

Forgiveness turned out to be the most powerful force for good in her life. Receiving and giving forgiveness can be a life-changing event in many of our lives as well. Is this what the Christian faith is all about? (Remember (Romans 8:31-19 and 1 John 3:20?) How does this relate to your faith life?

Chapter 27: "independence Day"

Tragic events in 1993 in Pakistan caused more outrage against Islamic Law and the oppression against Christians.

What results when love and joy is gone and fear takes over? What does fear lead to? (middle of page 159)?

The political and religious environment in Pakistan helped make a rift between Victoria and her brother.

Then the day came when the family decided that for business it was time to move to live in America. Life in America was wonderful for the first year or so with its freedom of religion and less prejudice. But then September 11, 2001, happened.

Chapter 28: "Judgment"

Fear, hate and anger began to creep back into Victoria' s heart as a result both of the feelings of Muslims and to feelings toward Muslims.

She discovered that in Pakistan differences in religion divided people, but in America it was difference in personal appearance that creates divides. What did she determine again would be her mission (middle of page 168)?

Victoria saw that even in America people tend to prejudge people on the basis of how they look, how they dress, and how they live. How could she get people to see the person and not just the outer appearance? Do you see this as an important issue? Can you recall making assumptions and judgments about people before getting to know them better?

Victoria began by talking to Bible study groups at her church. She said that terrorists accomplished one of their purposes by getting Americans to fear, even hate, each other.

How did she compare book covers to people (page 172)?

Chapter 29: "Her Voce of Faith"

Victoria was able to found a new mission society, "Voice of Faith." She felt accepted and welcomed among this new multi-ethnic group. She prospered in the new realization of her faith mission. By learning through life to overcome her own fears and anger issues she became able to help others see how they could do the same.

Victoria met Raj while delayed at an airport. Both were from Pakistan so they had much in common to converse about, but he was an atheist and she was a Christian. She gave him a Bible and in time he read it and became a Christian. Her experiences had given her the courage to speak up about her Christian faith and be used by the Holy Spirit to see others come to faith in Christ.

How often have we heard about people coming to faith in Christ through their reading of the Bible? From your experience, can you explain how it happens?

Victoria says that her grandfather had taught that our love for each other should transcend religion. What did her stumbles along the course of her life finally help her to overcome (bottom of page 170)?

Do you agree that Jesus' love and forgiveness may be the most powerful force in the world? What do you feel that powerful force has accomplished? Explain.

Jesus is the bridge from this life to eternity. He is also the bridge of love between people. Through Jesus we can look beyond our religions and cultural differences to establish trusting and loving relationships.

Some Christians feel that they are under attack in western societies, so they lash out in fear, anger and even violence. What does Victoria's story tell us about such hatred?

Do you think that if we too have to go through trials and persecutions like Victoria, will we reject hatred and do as Jesus says, "Love your enemies, and pray for those who persecute you." (Matthew 5:46; Luke 18:8)?

To see a video interview with "Victoria," go to

https://missionnationpublishing.com/would-you-love-a-muslim-neighbor

In the video interview "Victoria" is called "Nor Hook "for reasons of safety.

To see more video interviews, resources for outreach to new ethnic groups, books for sale and information on a book display for biographies of missionaries go to
www.MissionNatinPublishing.org

Made in the USA
Monee, IL
10 June 2026

52191936R00024